PULMONÍA

John M. Bennett

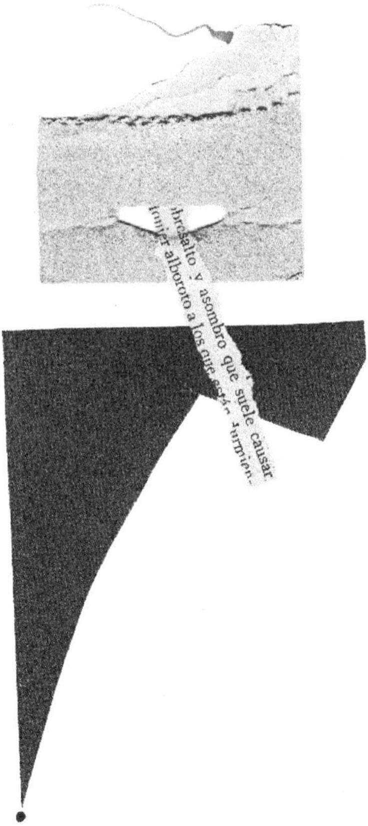

LUNA BISONTE PRODS
2023

PULMONÍA

John M. Bennett

May 2017 - January 2018

Some of these poems use the Hicucu form
invented by Jim Leftwich in 2014. In Leftwich's words,
"A Hicucu has three lines.
Each line has three syllables.
Each syllable has an unspecified number of mutagens, or letters."

Some of these poems have appeared in the following venues:
The In-Appropriated Press, Otoliths, Naked Sunfish, Utsanga, Pense Aqui, Uut Poetry, Angry Old Man, Caliban Online, Ffwl Lleuw, PBW, Bagazine, Surrealists and Outsiders, Hay(na)ku, and *Brave New Word.*
Apologies for any omissions!

Back cover photo & book design by C. Mehrl Bennett

ISBN 9781938521881

LBP

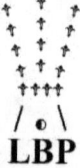

Luna Bisonte Prods
137 Leland Ave
Columbus OH 43214 USA

imposible

invisibles los pel
daños un humo mo
jado uh t tap
on the sh shoulder
a round a cor ner

a

shoe falls into a gutter

wind

to wet
a towel

a dog a
fork

el albañil

bBrick a foRm
de es cencia SENT
IENCE a ghast's pul
món ar enoso disparaître
et apparaître à nouveau
)*S. Beckett*(encore à une
nouvelle lugar de DIA
MANTES after
eats the storm rolling
in yr shirt my Trou
bled Towel sl
ides down ay pared
pis ante *mur de mer*
de yr iffy shoe
picante pues

f'ing stone...

asweep

the p LUNGE r gozne
sin ABRIR la puerta sin
luz cae POR LA ES
CALERA wear I slept a
sleep a déjà été employé
(*M. Boinvilliers*) yr Long False
Step à écrire les difficultés
invisibles que me aciegan
so I see dust burning
in the Corners where the
wind folds its breath

issue me ,*the twisted broom*

eleguá

cLustered in a Neck
yr fog snail ,creep
beside a lens ah
Turnabout ah mes
pieds c'est la nuit
(*J-M de Heredia*) yr
SOGGY FORK uh
hull up sloshed be
side's the Clotted
Lunch sleeping in
yr THroat tu perro
muerto al acecho
detrás de la puerta

indemne the louder mist

breast stroke

the reef the
reach the
ratty arm

flinks

sigh lens the sh
ort c law DOUBTS
yr scene neck *point*
d'air YO ME ABRÍ
EL BRAZO fulan
minante dans le
miroir des sables
)*J-M de Heredia*(su
sodicho s wore the
TOOTH OFF wh
ispered h air kno
tting in yr clouds
ah flop offf s
leep's uh focused

light retraction ,
ended's sheet

embolder

mot h m
outh 's
ilencio il
eso ,es e

foretext

f eel me f eet o
hendoscopic ssnnore
RELAPSANT ARMPIT
an yr rendospoon où
fuit un char de feu
)*J-M de Heredia*('s hot
ice replied yr eyes
seal my teeth yr
whirl relearned a Boy
Soaked SWEATA
LACKE ay siezure
siezed a fork di
vision ! ni vista
genética crece ni
sonido soñado *the*
puzzle fogs and
dribbles on the floor

livre vacarme

dung fired a
dumpster r
ed itioned's
shriek a page
D

—¡Fuego, fuego!
despertaron a los dormidos pasajeros con

runny throne

aged the stinking itch be
neat yr shirt foam sp
urts out yr chest yr g
runted thigh ,voice remains
,yr neck flood's case of
HOPPING THRONE useless
door a bashed machine c
latters across the sleepless
street before each sill a
heap of orange shit burns
)*called yr face*(charred mirror
multitud sin huesos en la
plaza una bandera constipada
un foco que me abre el fuego

la diarrea

no me hables no me
abras no me cierres súbeme
la escalerita con pan tos
tado bájame el calzón
sucio de mis recuerdos
antiguos antiguallas del
temor invisible que veo
sin titubeos sin roteiros
fulmino mis ocurrencias
fumigo tus habladurías
fustigo las páginas carra
spadas en el pozo de
mi sombra poniente y me
fla fla flaqueo al ras de mi
gogordura incipiente

...et toujours se taira.
- Alfred de Vigny

malade

mud and nuts / ah hammer
g ate a seaslug fog's
water FASTER THIN yr
y ear scrawls in ,la
semilla biologique j am
med deep in yr nose .un
tie the hose yr fork im
pales before a HINGE
sleeps beneath a ladder b
arcs and b arks ,fed
the fango en famille's E
GGS C RACKED in
yr shshorts ,w ashed *at once*

His nuts on his neck.
- Blaster Al Ackerman

prélude

salad of knives and corks
yr WINDY SHIRT b ashed
'is 'ead in de serves a
c hair sp lit inna carwreck
was my mirror and wall
et's useless frothing of
FILTHY LUCRE is yr
locker flooded in a basement ?
)*paychecks faded in pink*
slime(.SLEEP THROUGH
THE DOOR a toxic cloud of h
air over yr bowl it writhes

nor ham nor rice nor flattened spoon

see now

nor has
a loop a
loup aff
reuse bu
t's a pool a
poul   et

rains

shud der
the pane
spelt d
rips your
pock et a
wet one

deconstrued

ring the neck your FIRE
lathed SOT GAZE see
thing hair muddies the
mirror yr lipgloss sm
eared Ay Tongue &
ChloroForm bees LOST
IN LIBRARIES' shel
ved vowels were sm
oking Butts and Buts
asleep next an ob
sidian blade yr
hand-writhen statue
without a single glyph
a museum rained at the
crossroads skin
hisses in a shirt

After Ivan Argüelles'
"Venus Deconstructed"

get up

stroked it up yr stumbled
neck float reified the
flaqueza soap ,fails to
verify ,TASTE OF KNOT
falls on crumpled deck
)*peed beneath the desk*(
shape of combs .sand
sheets down the mirror
your spit clouds in
,ice and play lock st
ones grind yr
HAND fog's offal
POKED RIGHT UP
off yr streaming face

bombs and steps meat
and wind ~ ~ ~ ~ ~ ~ ~

influido

same dream of eating the
tick ets ma mer de sable
EACH OUCH undoored ah
floor compaction ,my swi
mming belt past toothy
rocks' gas retension tu
mono muerto en los re
molinos sin salida)*A. Di*
Benedetto(del muelle's mou
thed numb ers masticados
and muddy muttering yr
named stream yr
feet s s ticking to air

defocus refocus surfocus a
flood murmurs über the hill

ste p

b its sho
e xit s
its a
w ay

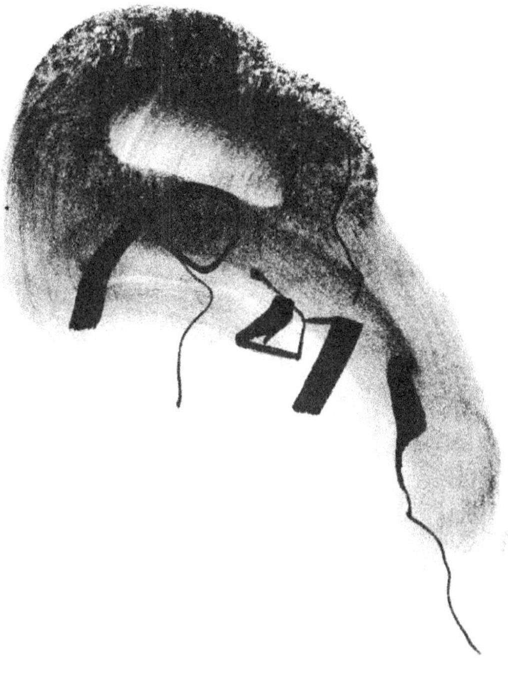

for tune

slaw mite sings yr
gas intestino in tensivo
que me puse guaje mi
col rajado ,son áta me
desátame in cantado in
sectívoro sudado en mi
camisa de hule ,humming
,torcido sorta ,said my
stunned shade resonation
,cells in my bursting mouth
.in shade the swallowed
chord a strangled sh
adow ,bursts from the
nether hole

embolismo ,bólido ,c
aught the breath

such

full of
bagger

out the itch

ringing

ddum Lankwidge mi
ssing's hot trigger ho
t grave L muddy in yr
backpocket's empty th
ought a sLeepy backwar
ds with a sandy arrow's
cLoudy like yr waves
of Linty hair broke pea
k's g Litter in some
we eds *a a   a   a*

After Ivan Argüelles
"Is Mud the Crown"

trans

roots in light
yr stem drain

yr face a sleep
in a bucket

o say o say

gotea el traje cacasi
olvidado mas no del lodo
misty leg below vines
said and said lourde et
diaphane explico y ex
plico deexplico tu me
déexpliques yr c
lick c lack spelling wheel
it's all bien dicho ya d
icho mal dic ho rror
inside yr slumbered c
loud dictionnaire sans
feuilles .tu me miras
la nariz ,con su dedo
baboso je dis je d is j
e di s

Je commence à regretter
le temps de ma machine à écrire
et son clic clac d'indépendantiste
- Ben Vautier

poissons

deux poissons sont morts
ils flottaient sur la surface
ils pesaient lourd)*Ben Vautier*(
yr SHOULDER SAND 's
same ripe stain EACH
FOG dime si no me re
pito EL PITO desinflado
yr HOT CLOUDY EYES re
versed in my HAH *name* is
g one awide *.heat my d*
reaming-shirt one sleeve
is cold yr swallowed
face returns the spit-on
b each birded sheet yr
huffing sleep drifts on

il n'y pas de vent solide

no it wasn't

dusted the cloud
reached the fork
named the shit

it was a storm form
it was not a cube
it was a shot shirt

I saw the soon
I saw it clammed
I saw what sighed

muttered in a spoon
nattered in a mirror
spit in a pocket

it was the coughing shoe
it was the misty leg
it was the swallowed book

)))garga...ojos(((

...g...arg...a...bruma;;; 's 's...lot...
...lun...ch;;;mu:::te 's 's 's...leet...
...dus...t;;;c...c...OW..!!!..d..im:::L...
:::eg...g???g...g...ut...d,,,ug,,,g,,,L...
...ett;;;uce,,,p...it,,,a,,,a,,,nt(((c...
,,,...law)))rud...der...g,,,g,,,]]]ate[[[...
""""s""""lim;;;f,,,f,,,ool...g...g...rime.,.,.,...
:::s...s...wal...e:::h:::ot...F:::F:::
...og///e///a/t///y...y...our:::H:::
:::H:::and...d...d...ot...J,,,J,,,ewel***...
...m(((M(((...ate...\\\l\\\l...ock...
...d...d,,,um)))c)))C...AW,,,f...| | |...
...ence| | |---s---s---w,,,eat;;;...'s's's""""
;;;v;;;v;;;en...d,,,ad~~~]O[~~~jos~~~

`...;;;...///...:::...=}}}}};;;{{{{{=---\\\;.,,,,,,,;.....'

regarder la brûme

lake of sot's gun he
ave yr fork out t hair tine's
fast sp lash il est tout mon
horizon)*Pierre Bonoit*(an
urinous moon sinks into yr
hand c'est la méthode gal
vanoplastique ma main te
touche les yeux PHONUL
GRAPHIQUES fog fills a
warehouse corpses wearing
just my shoes ;;;;;;;;;;;;;;;;;;;;;;;;;;;;;;;;;;
YOUR MOUTH BOAT wr
istless on a grassy field's yr
face breathes out breathes
out))))))))))))) s s s
tumbles on a single step

...senda o nudo...

usher

endictive shed ,the roof
smoke's rise and mind the
,burning tree yr ,neck river's
sodden wall | | swallow a
comb yr frog mask mel
ts off you'll see the h
ole aginous bright with
ink .redetectif swarm ,fe
et musgo en llamas 's m
y s nore s luffed a way
ay lonely sleep mine's l
eft a foot blind stroke a
turning , , , , , , ,

y

h h inge
in
gle
d
awn's rust

LL

c l aw
e d ust
h ead
o u t

i

now raised

s un s kin s lides acr
oss a vow el bow l c
racked a radiant b
ank le's light dar
kens yr sky's rock
broke broke door
behind]cornered w
all invistive pre
sence decomposing
was a stre
aming M O *O* N

Twitching in Ivan Argüelles'
"Fragment Temple Ruins"

wwindd

enter ,flees
the sleeper less

the trees

dawn milk

hump and shut ro
ugh key yr net s
lipped out a greasy
stone it was ,f
illed your hand loss
defiled the nested
air .upper smoke
led your doom led
your fiery light
was lumped and free

cuddled ,curdles space

ediface

pee l a ch
eek
ack
sl eep stool

underglare

nutter game fr ought
crow d yr b ranches
shshake ,my ashy
hole read Lunch
turns across a p
late fork bent s
iezed FREE THE
TINE yr s lack n
eck toeplasm scores
an scores oh Lurch
LAME ENSLABMENT
puzzles in the wrist
puzzle of the.......”

worm cloud

- For Aaron Flores &
Shawn McMurtagh

yr fface h ash *sieze*
the wall CLOUDS OR
WORMS blank thing
lunched through CRAW
LING SCREEN ha hoff
HOT SOON debrides
yr shirt ,foggy soap
seeps out yr MASK
WASP time to c
law drinking skin ah
final lake's heap of
dying fish CACANUBES
que me salen deexplicadas
desaguadas reinconstipadas
de *lo deintestinal que me*
inpronuncia el nnombre

not

yap a minute
floor a minute
time a minute

a

she a bark
water she a
flooded root
a

¡no ,no puedes!

mind the time yr k
not's collapsed deBATE
a shore thing re
fogged your sNAIL sm
oking up your sleeve's
SLIME ARM ,inreactant
leached a pAGE
infogdent's sloppy wall
et)*again*(sanded
to a shine .tus
huevos dereinfectantes
que te duermen en el
papantalón)*Pantaleone*
que te ronca en la
dermis caracal(
¡ábrame ,muérdame ,no
te permito leerme!

fundus

fondo caminante
nalga de humo
nalga de agua
tumbo ambiguo

revueltos

es peso es
misto es al
mohada es
no es huevo
yema es

caucho

intacta mi coatlicue
adormida adrede
dedespierto mi ojo de
recho ,roncante el
siniestro ,PLUMAS
DE HULE que te
enguantizan la mano
¡cuánta bruma que
veo! con mi códice
ensucio el agua ,es
pejo embalsamado tu
página desencarnada es
un guía de autobuses
perdidos por la frontera
,humo negro que
sube y una tormenta
que baja :entre ellos
una llanta calva *tu len gua er a*

Et pour que sa beauté soit plus terrible encor,
Casque ses blonds cheveux de quelque bête ailée
Et fait bomber son sein sous la gorgone d'or.
-José-María de Heredia

ether matter

mountain word
canal word
name word

leaf an alphabet
leaf an echo
leaf emerge

was fear in a trunk
was bees in light
was silenced glass

sleep beside wind
rust above wind
thunder under wind

torn rags or mirror
torn breath or crevice
torn page or ants

Inhaled from Ivan Argüelles'
"Eschatology"

arena

bull no d
e w r ought
hung s
word lun
g r ass

can't see

pulse tube
if wore imb
alance d

d ry f og

slip

sho e n
or sho
re kno
w n ot a
s t e p

even

s ore a s well
r am a do
or fire
a ffly

~*~

open up

swollen door
a cheek th
inks in mou
the ,the knoB

TIME TO FOOT

name your foot on the courthouse lawn
dry your foot on the mumbling face
seize your foot as it turns the key
flag your foot as it smears a mask on the grass
lay your foot in the cornered cloud
raise your foot to the blooded mirror
time your foot to the strategic decision
flay your foot before the smirking screen
swallow your foot as the books are flushed
desock your foot as the ballots burn
write your foot as the parade dissolves
shout your foot as the committee slides to the floor
do not gag your foot as the dogs approach
phone your foot as it surrounds the pool
breathe your foot in a penciled kitchen
rain your foot on the drought in the halls
brain your foot on the thoughtless steps
hat your foot as the ash descends
tongue your foot in the blooming graves
wash your foot in the crowded window
praise your foot as the walls become air

foot and shirt relimber me
foot and stone embellish me
foot and sea unpolish me
foot and headache open me

roots of fog

the fog net shed
the ash font spewed
the chair sweat cracked

spelling door it said
folding hair it said
crawling book it said

fingers in mud
crackers in a fencerow
coffee in the gasoline

cough your shadow out a window
burn your list out a window
count one air out a window

a storm framed the temple
a stage burned at dusk
a tree slept all night

was

pee and climb
the rest ,
nor mind

vibe

pulsor
inflopt
g outs

brilliance

the luckiest day is your
throat 's st rong sewer
muscled u p yr leg 's h hot
FOG UP THERE 's
stem sn aps off *f inger*
is yr sleep 's l ong h ánd
dale ¡cómete las plu mas
plurilactosas! ≈ suerte de
fango es ,y la muerte de la
mano es critora criptomán
tica , cri cri sis temática de lo
que sé no sé ,no me trago el
día ése ,h ours of frag rant fe
cal mur murs oozing from the
sky's blue screen

C'est ruiner l'ombre quotidienne
Sur des sommets perpétuels
- Paul Éluard

porc

shud der i
t of f ***h***
ung clou

D

hale

fog or knot
or not
,bed ,lunch
,lung

clalm

shirt clam
calm ,dirt
,fuzz and ’
s cream

dig

c leave a
for kk
tine to c
hew sp
lit mine

pocket lint burial

bury your pocket lint
bury your whistled air
bury your foggy mask

salami in wind
tongue in wind
socks in wind

name a tree some time
fold a shirt last week
forget the swallowed fork

road or book
lung or book
mirror and book

is rain or was
is fingered pin
is rats a head

was you was I

I bubbled "in my shirt"
nod and left ,right be
fore the ash cloud
rised ,retained a shape
endured some dribbly fog a
,bag of cheetos smoulders
in the basement UNDER
STAIRS your rustling
cheek your CHEWS AND
CHEWS a doubled spoon
A DOUBLE SPOON *st*
ir yr ant nest read the
swarming chains yr sleeves
pulse with legs *ah ah*
pile you leak and leak *a*
red shade wheezed inside yr thigh

ant meat nest

where a nostril cross a
face swims a doorknob
blooms with grease is
ribless chains a
chair against the wall SIT
AND CHIN say nothing eve
ry voiced shoe sh
uffling toward your sou
p's clotted whistle oh
chew your glove thrust
that ant meat nest ,fi
ngered thinly through
your roach-stained pages
● ● holes and fingernails em
bedded in the binding((((

it and not ,windy sandwich

limb

boom storm chase a
declawed cat a plas
tic wallet with yr
dollar jerky where
yr spoon deformed
where yr neck tower
strangled in a sneeze
hose snaking out
the flatscreen it's
yr cheese doodle fire
your PRECIOUS WORM

)melt and learn(

los pasos perdidos

I am not your foot *)D. Lynch(*
for all yr ashy needs cum
breabismo lock dog show sw
eat sleep fistula was your
daily rice INHALE THE
FOG was wilted soup step
away the snore's bang light
seeming drip ' ' '// nor shoe
beneath the beach a
temple ,lonely groan a
THTHUNDER'S backitch
flood I am not the walk
foot I am not not and
flood your second floor I am
not your second floor so
easy rumbled past a neck cr
eeping out the b eded neck's
skull-hung ::dim mu d d
rains be tween yr socks ,em
bandaged sammich *am yr*
steep claw grease

Ni ma gorge de son silence
- Paul Éluard

do

,is ,bore ,nut
latch or f
lame ,step
out any way

see s not

ramboid
ut tur
n a way

not

shoul d uck
duke it sn
out shou
ld ld ld

si soy

,run ,fog ,bite
numb er neck
,caw ,flow ,di
me

sin e

in capaz fr ente al p
ayaso défumé *on le frappe*
beaucoup en lisant le texte
imprimé)F. G.-L.(my
shirt ripped said *pay aso ase*
sino dribbled in a rain a
mirror under water was ton
pied tu zapatón una pied ra
es ines encia ,viajo por un es
pacio el mismo esp acio
siempre "donde" moras "d
onde" mueres despierto tu
cabezpejo en que no te ves
a wall of blood a corpse st
roke your hand *un e muet*
à fin de son prénom)F. G.-L.(
si lenc you commenc
qu lo dic todo

sans tentative de traduction
- Frédérique Guétat-Liviani

pud dle

mirror a sh
ard a bove
rain st
rung
ton gue yr nose

ton e

ate the h at
ate the p low
ate the st one
ate the an t

l'informé

il pleur o
vídate li
quaste pl
uma in r
espira da

for sure

plositive je su
is)hacia a
dentro(I'm a
inbomber

nor in nor out

endogenous flashes in my
coffin glue and saw a
dust-deep bed bu
rsts beneath my eye *You*
with water to rise by
falling tissue dance en
visioned as a blank un
libro torturado como car
ne de lavandería churns
was *We at the roots of*
doors the windows exogenous
foaming saw *You in the blood*
of envelopes me in the flo
oded hope could see *a*
lightproof pod of songs was
oil hosing from the dark anus
was the basement steps the cra
ckling concrete floor was my
face in sssleep

With lines from Jim Leftwich,
Synonymous Pronoun Poems, 1993

dim frame

sh
outed
sh sh
adow

)you said(

hand it

grim grin
or g love

col

off er soon
a bellum
lapse
dead salad

paisaje

under the blubber wold
wall or knife an absence
essential abscesential see
ps behind yr eye sees
a b one c locked among
red trees sunk over the
hill ASH TOWER we
t gr ease slat upon a
thr one forking day WH
AT BURNS IS SEEN
turns and flees

lo de ella

d rip a do
or ,que
me pus e
mu do mu
ét *her*

lecho

swollen dream
nalga dream
mooseneck dream
leche dream

wake not

sleep and short
sleep and wall
sleep and stun

the outer cloud
the inner lake
the other spoon

is nor was
cream nor fall
bomb nor think

pencil in air
tongue in air
shoe in air

glass break is
window hair is
grave **L** step is

arroyo

bor bot eo
no es nu be
il pleur je
su is ni sa is

aug

te mi do la
ca ra te to
co la len
gua gua gua

Deinterpretations

The dream of a barbecue in a bathhouse
is the dream of a stone roasting over a
coal-filled hole in the ground, which is
the dream of a cloud or a
fist full of cheese

...of a dream of Josh Ronsen

The dream of an adopted baby is the
dream of a bowl of cherries spinning
on a kitchen table; the dream of the
bowl saying "are you my coconut
peanut dad" is the dream of a
sidewalk going downhill entering
a sea of burning bottles

...of a dream of Bibiana Padilla Maltos

The guilt upon leaving an empty
swimming pool is the joy you feel
when filling your pockets with smoke

...of a guilt of Antic Ham

just an eye

a fish's luminescent sleep
a mind's sand river
a cloud's plutonium thread

asterisks cluster on a waist
commas flicker on a skin
periods iterate in the azure

is descendant moth
is rudderless surf
is transparent labyrinth

lamination of a breeze
hollowing of a book
longing of a hand

the slashing of an eye
the ladder of an eye
the sentence of an eye

After Ivan Argüelles'
"variations on a line" & "poet, the"

comandaterio

rice risen in your hat a
doubled fork wet in
cision *in your wallet's*
gore each containment
shoulders all that gas was
liquid standing on your
hairs was ash imper ative
in your book's remote
control spit a tongue-sm
eared pen was clean or th
inking-mask was ripppling
down your face *in a dry bowl's*
sudden wave

wisdom storm ,angle of yr fat

dude

mud through
out the chain
endorsal loss
your bright
“flooded collar”

mayo

beach mind
dactile dog s
crawl ,sand
...............glue

babababosojo

llueve tu pierna
un lente es
sans yeux s
ans spit

HICUCU ONE

nube lent
es cen cia
invista

twink ex cre
scence fry me
up one off

limonda
me hierba
si vague d'eau

poco pas
ado r mi
do est oy

pus tu len
cia lengua's
flatulence

cumbre in
visible
]sót ano[

sabor de
sable ar
enoso

HICUCU TWO

underwha
cker ben dit
grips fog meal

pezcojer
trembalar
dondear

seep a shoe
sole tongue float
shadow leaks

chump and kneed
clockless thumb
ghost you chew

invoke fly
shorter lung
in nor out

tu sans yeux
j'ai une dent
nez mais non

rumbo fla
co merme
adrede

alrede
dor mido
aire soy

subo ,co
mo ,muero
,inmerso

rana es
bubo es
no está

tu descends
je rentre
disparâitre

fork faucet
"ask a cow"
eaten name

For C. Mehrl Bennett

utter able

able to unburn
able to inane
able to impale

a wind remembered
a hole remembered
a still remembered

your damp bucket
his damp window
her damp tongue

is stone unburied
was ink unburied
hand unburied

utter through the forest
utter hissing faucet
utter silence drinks your head

beatus ille

wetness cloud my f
ork thrasher time *La*
rivière que j'ai sous la
langue *)P. Éluard(* c'est
n'est pas que lourde my
cargo pants shaking on the
ferris wheel yr short
shot tomb stuffed with
grass *"jambes de pierre"*
)P.É.(knotty smoke fumée
I SWALLOWED THE
FUSE your short dog
barked ,an oof ***W***
ancid in's ***R*** 's b lunt
ir ***A*** dryness whirring thru a
cicada's wings yr watch tos
ses t urns sin sesos et
Je glisse sur le toit des mers
)P.É.(la lengua es lluvia
en san gre tada

je ne vois plus l'empreinte
- Paul Éluard

HICUCU THREE

dots and dance
nor flaky
was nor not

chew haw limb
meater shoe
yr blam ding

myth and log
torn shovel
languid grime

nor knot nor
paw asleep
is ash an

le mot ay
ay le mot
motile ,eh

chimney neck
case flubber
frog detail

eat the brick
powder hump
now engage

in's blubber
in's thumb mind
raw cash inch

tub and lung
nostril plug
swallow spoon

lick the pole
offal slab
knife debate

shift your itch
finger drawn
bluster death

other blabs
me a mute
your hog chokes

HICUCU FOUR

ex plode ex
plain exude
ex dorm ant

c hip or c hop
es moco
“exilio”

should count fart
number ass
fecal wig

mud norm pul
gar bled use
less write sticks

bust it off
why gently
screw the shit

book mutt or
roof roof sped
off choking

no me dig
as pirin
a bé bé

tore it out
flopping was
sidewalk moon

simper feed
shuddered lunch
convection

gas and hall
foot and leash
blood and rust

gagging lunch
your shoulder
's foggy load

crust of sky
crumb I saw
falling knife

hell's light

your gassy coil
your other vowels
your strangled drum

shirts of air
walls of air
ombre d'air

draw down hips
damp down silence
map down drowning

sweaty tongue in river
asbestos song in river
vacuumed light in river

is hair or sandwich
is loam or echo
is sleep or empty

Meandering through Ivan Argüelles'
"Ombre d'Inferno"

nulopendio

swim contamination *La rivière*
que j'ai sous la langue)Paul
Éluard(CHEW MY CRUMBS
your drifting s m o k e my
ton que te abre lo serrado)c
hunk fell off(your CREEPING
TEETH dis lodged in rapids'
mouth thick with cheese
said yr pocket's rusty nails la
nada que he comido end your
gagg end the sausage slith
ered through grass *it's*
a nostril you see th rough
MISTURANZA DE MOCO
flail through the spinal sew
age it's yr time compaction ,sure

Toits rouges fondez sous la langue
- Paul Éluard

HICUCU FIVE

clip my dia
mónd ame
músculo

misty chump
grunt detail
bring the frog

rustle snake
fangoid breath
snore impaled

chip chop shape
sees the fork
slake clot spit

means mind half
drip and snore
clean spine laughs

sot pork grin
was stun was
thin door clouds

rendered wall
loud crack stirred
heard the cough

sugar dime
spread a hunch
wind up gut

unless bread
unless gas
unless phone

bileless strewn
evil ham
rotting door

utter gate
mobbed a leg
twitching bone

bray feets spray
throne olive
sinks away

HIHICUTCUT

bubble upper
mute adoption
speeds and dribbles
swish and foggy

stink arises
double stubble
close yr face rash
opens earache

sweat relinquished
time of sleep names
swallows hash lot
greasy mail wakes

bloat now contained
river gargled
was time you snored
shadowed with gnats

will dig remember

I was torn to
morrow I was
born tomorrow
I was water

itch and throat or
cough and miss will
seem to flag a
cross next week was

shaped pocket lint
burnt the pages
float by dock in
pool of lentils

fog before eye glass
wall returns last
week the shovels
rust under clay

lugar ameno

spread corn's cool worm
taste air's gas fumes
shorter dog than
steps beneath tree

exits wind out
sunflower is
forgot monday
looms through fog

gasp and think too
much draw a sphere
your forehead's light
switch off it on

a stump your hand
a leaf your neck
a stick your tongue
a seed your shoe

lo mojado

evade the crawl
or voided shirts
imbue your face
with blood-soaked dirt

it's ash and corn
it's soap or foam
busted screen or
glass stuck in bone

dripping drink and
sharded bright meat
licked off the door
swallowed in heat

inch across mud
mumble in weeds
eye always closed
fluid what sees

dead at least

I said yr faucet *Quelques secondes de silence)Lucien Suel(* tongued thru a
rain my back remembers last Monday
FEET BURIED IN GRAVEL what
coughing sky relaxant *b ack yar d*
strewn with gears you a dribbling
shut shirt *db db db db db*)shadow
of the "great condensation"(pearled
on yr tines' ab negation ab stention ab
domenation AB OMINABLE trick
les fired water ,said your thoughtless
said your lunge through the pane sa
id sack of embers said of you "you
carried a mouth at least"

...rouler sa langue dans sa bouche...
- Savoir-vivre & bonnes manières,
2009 (Esprit XVIIIe)

HICUCU SIX

invade a
dog recloud
master rain

lip a fork
clip a seed
shit a not

wet ring fog
tube enforced
blind in slaw

install a
hurt tooth face
nor resolve

shutter my
neck's swallow
arfy pants

liberate
sock inhales
dandruff time

plod and grin
sleep a mile
nasal tear

fantod ,rice
plato es
sodden ,mice

change the dot
below an
empty name

greet black mist
mind the stone
break your feet

grabbed your ash
opened her
door a flash

page or crust
crumbled switch
where a wall

end meat

vision of the hammered phone
beside your sleep tidy
cereal skull giggles like a
broom if broom unlike your
swallowed sore were wind *is*
wind is shallow thunder
of yr creeping conscious *scious*
scious wall MY FINGER
SAID your verso's silence
. . . . .)plumber's dream
of dog bowels(it's the b
arking hand .*wheel wheel*
wheel wheel wheel wheel
wheel crashing loose on the
the far side of the road

drip and glory ,your finger burnt

HICUCU SEVEN

- For C. Mehrl Bennett

engineer
ábrame
el aire

thimbled breast
pillow dust
kiss my ,yes

stunted pig
travesty
dropped gun off

been a clown
shat dog bowl
laugh and spit

dripping tooth
“insurance”
gag in sack

but but but
wrong path snore
tub tub tub

lunch bit down
shy cloud mind
suck a fork

trouble ouch
end of time
ow ow ow

what crash said
nor issue
fart ahead

table grunt
see your shoe
open sole

bum bum bum
bat bat bat
sot sot sot

phone your cheese
ask a cow
shattered nail

reflet du ciel

roofless she a float con
densed *fileuse/mot fondant*
)Paul Éluard(SAID A NECK
redoubled at a keyboard
Rien cette chair fait de
peu)P.E.(la calavera “nada”
me piensa me pesa me pis
a h bootless she my dirty
wheel was warped and shit
,her long yarn sp ins
melts your sounded shirt
)doubles in the fog('s it
chy shout dries yr sil
enced encía depronounced
deentombed she or you was
none was spoke beneath the
smoke's descension

Aux yeux nourris de son miroir
- Paul Éluard

HICUCU EIGHT

fusilar
recaer
respirar

queso que
cae lento
bócame

sueño sor
do mir es
cuintle

agarrar
manguera
cuello es

bisturí
infantil
ombligal

efectivo
sin efec
tó mame

masticar
la luna
escupir

es culo
es cape
es se es

símbolo
boli fón
gárgaras

sumo su
do rmirte
substrato

bala de
aire ag
ujero

muero sin
morir vi
vo sin ver

wetness

il y a des fleuves *que j'ai tourné*
et retourné cinq ou six nuits dans
ma tête)M. Boinvilliers(streaked
out my pants a leg égale ,a bank's
shiny weeds el desayuno que ya
echará espuma is yr dental
superstructure ,lunch and fog
)fog ahead behind(a he ad be
hind er gone the window cr
acking shut SPELT A RINGING
PHONE is was the crown *yr shoe a*
wave ≈toward uh ba ckw ash≈ "my
arms held you" mud sweeps across
your sidewalk)more than six the
nights not yet ends(*a can of beans*
glinting on the windowsill // // // // //

La rivière que j'ai sous la langue,
L'eau qu'on n'imagine pas...
- Paul Éluard

HICUCU NINE

chew clock waste
in back flow
oh wall out

temp us fid
git cluster
cave behind

read and leap
a plan door
coughing shut

plus valía
menos mal
mirada

mis tunas
mis manos
recuerdo

hot pliers
wet wallet
stun swallowed

meat the mist
escombros
j'ai mangé

cochon pol
itique ar
bre qui brûle

pesantez
peldaño
con caca

weeds and lunch
ringing phone
one or none

doggèd mute
reap the fog
silence said

it it it
ch ch ch
it ch it

merdeurtre

...je devrais bientôt me taire *)Paul Éluard(*
mas el sol me sube en el ojo an other
dday headaches across my scalp mais les
bombes respirent sous le lit *MERDRE ME*
URTRE MERDRE MEURTRE MERDRE
MEURTRE a bee thrashes in the wet sink *zz*
zb zzzb zzzb tourbillon d'hilarité et d'horreur
)Stéphane Mallarmé(I licked yr face its
faucet's high squeal sleeps beside your
cheek dark room grey coffin of the open
door SHUT THE FUCK UP leggjjerk
under the sheet yr cloud come down yr
breath a nest of sticky webs *tongues air*
silenced leaving "arriver est un départ" *)P.E.(*
no estoy aquí ni soy estaré ayer ay er ror rim's
streaming glass inimbalanced inimixturable

Le mot fenêtre un mur le bouche
- Paul Éluard

HICUCU TEN

soupir le
fenêtre
inourverte

me puse tu
camisa e
vaporé

choose shit sheet
choose shore shot
loose sand stuns

commotion
muddy sleep
water rise

hervirte
cogote
despierto

fool nodder
knot the cord
pull too tight

middle neck
outer shoe
blaster key

drippy thing
seated lunch
affaire morte

lube tube gut
tomb vacía
meat to come

shorter wave
lurch off page
it fuck it

plume sêche
pinga wet
porte en feu

chew yr pants
choke yr book
change yr skull

hack it off

page of corn que me he comido
,lustros ha   *;*   *oh consolante horreur*   *!*
)Chaussepierre(my face mask's sw
irling hair's the stream your voice was th
ick THOUGHT THE THOUGHTLESS
TEETH and gravel   *;*   *la bouche ouverte,*
,   *,*   *,*   *,* *)Chaussepierre(* “I twisted
back my eyes” your naked saw ,chain of
mice crosses room gets lost in the hall
)page of storm(*!*   *,*   *;*   *dans la*
coupe *)Chaussepierre(* alguna cosita no vista
ví ,la ventan a bierta un fue fuego fué o
aalaa page of form tongue climbs the wall
que conozco que no he conocido thum
b rain pounds my greasy specs my
hand's cut off ,g rasping *a a i i r r*

, ,   les entrailles   ,   ?rien
- Charles-Georges Coqueley de Chaussepierre

vent de merde

shorn meats a strangled door
Grave des mots avec un clou
)Th. Gautier(ce n'est rien mais
quelque chose condensed rechewed
ébranlé sourdement ha dicho ,clos
et crammed with socks your
negck reblooded ,steaks on phone
dripping said yr NOM RAUQUE
spat screen un libro vacío o
blanco de escuchpitazos anhelados
where a dog wind swirls teething
the knob's "sit on a distant lake"
your statue burns on the shore
your statue splits its head your
statue drowns in its shoe ≈≈≈
hairless and birdshat FEUILLE
OUBLIÉE ¿de quién es la
cara que escribo? ¿de quién son las
ascuas que tomo con mi café espresso?

leaf or shirt wword or tturd

la salida

lamento el túnel que me
devuelve un túnel lleno de libros
under my shirt a boat returns
spills its pages a greasy
shore it's what you read it's
what you never read crawling
laundry past the windows ou
les nuages ,n'importe ,it's a
green mist red streaked ,teléfono
sin auricular ,piedra o ham
burgüesa ,peldaño invisible
en el fondo del agua ,aguas
de risa al revés the entry
whistles and moans

N'AURA EU LIEU
- Stéphane Mallarmé

the madding

in maze of s inks your corn pool
cette coup de lait pur)Paul Éluard(
mis ojos mixtos ,monstres dans le
sable les chaussures vides in haze yr
th inks cornered with her socks
SCRAWLED WITH SHOULDER
GLUE *une façade affreuse* / |
\ , ; ’ ’ sin viento ,facial milk a
wave or grime *yr book drinks yr*
sweated hat will drunk have 
“corporate fascism” luggage stuffed
with tongues or form drool is your
wallet hammered with a nose is
your cellphone chewed with b lack
ra dish is your will have swallowed
la cara de rana con lápices flojos
como sopa seca

Et c'est aux foules de comprendre
La faiblesse des meurtriers.
- Paul Éluard

HICUCU HACKS

shlort flogic
if spider
langkuage by

alien hhunt
voice ungrown
ttent or hhead

liberat
or breeathing
genectic

words latdder
angngular
roots exsist

sentience coat
es shaking
absince' dis

tant reason
pro cess trees'
slecond tlongue

After Jim Leftwich's
Hicucu from Code of Signals

HICUCU VOID

void un veiled
mind dis persed
pool un seen

lethe flows
ampersand's
window lost

brain submerged
film undone
e van es

cent ch amber
rearing up
fingers flare

mask unspliced
your voices
shapeless grass

leaf evolved
chthonic
thumb or brain

into sea's
unending
thought event

unseen pool
dispersed mind
veiled the void

Found in Ivan Argüelles'
"Into the Lethe"

your forking tongue

chew the snake your coat
inhales ah twisted horn your
mouth unveils the blinding
comb or scissored cheek a
check against what time re
turns your first dead word
at last the end rethrives and
woofs *stone ape wood cloud*
your shoulder snaps your sm
oldered lunch BURNS THE
HORIZON . . . . shoe
thins in evening breeze

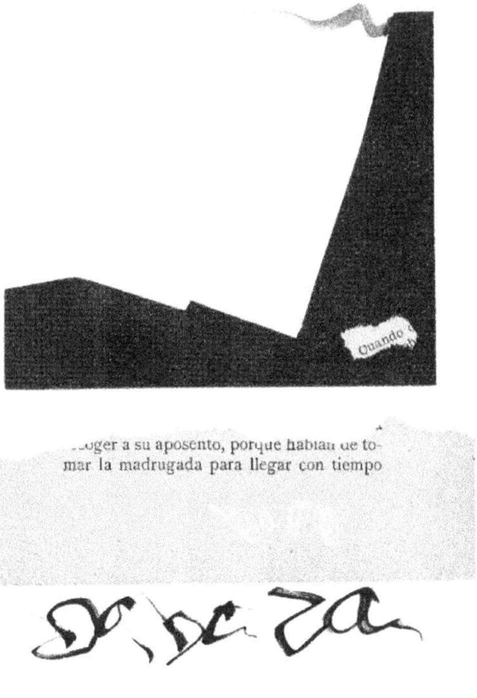

natación

twist my lake and cough
cough up sand *retrete*
inescuso swam up to you
wharf swarms with dogs
.my listed face your sl
uffing arms smattered
in the gritty fog *:;:;:;:;:;:;:;:;:;:;*
sendas hormigas que no
sé dónde formir clammed
up not snored *.outer ouch*
inner floor ,splinters and
olive pits récamara SIN
SALIDA escrita en tus
párpados de hule

aux écumes originelles
naguères d'ou sursauta son délire...
-Stéphane Mallermé

ojogrifo

Les beaux muscles de fer de
son corps surhumain)*José-María de*
Heredia(splinter off the water
TORMENTA DE LUZ my eye
s tabs and *bsats zzz* the comb
FELL OFF YOUR FACE tu
lupa sinks in the lake tiny
flames crinkle on the shore *n'ont*
pas brûlé ta chair fissure ,skin
sandwich ,trickles in the bowl
its muddy blond wig beneath a
garbage can it was yr last d
renched laundry failure gleaming
faucet o ojógrifo your shut
tered head turns in toward
me your rust and drowned moths
:*Il palpite, il frémit d'esperance et*
de fièvre ,tastes what drips
off down the drain

HICUCUCU La Piedra

knack of shim
mer où les
yeux s'en brûle

cheap stunt light
fame or flame
lock lock lock

martillo
sur mes pieds
sang no hay

flavor flab
flovar balf
alba of

drink this ttooll
is wok want
for nuttin'

it es il
list ie ie
nada es ¿no?

cosa tún
emetic
chain swallow

tepetl ,roof
stone release
your last tooth

I died I
stormed I
ate a wall

gr unt nur
egulate
simpathic

shutter cloud
open fog
clou de chair

lously hangs
final drip
sauce of guns

eats

your shirt I drilled it when
a grub doubled in the sink your
foot a cloud returns was
faucet leak again next Tuesday
loss of buttons and a headache
was a red pill a blue a hollow
pill – *your head of state* -
sodden clump drowning in the
shallows your leg it was
bent straight down no *we*
there no pastel towel mono
grammed with toothpaste I
slept inside your pocket
dreamed a runny fork that
dream the dream of starting
dinner over

was squirming in your cheek

echo

in in in
nur nur nur
nod nor nil

stew

in flate uh
hop boil

your leg

run away

cheese grew
sock shrank
dim tool

yum

your molar clock
hush it in
uk
chew

ok

moist drain
shut up

ass ash

finangle soap
duds rely
on piss detail

so eat

urinescent

Encore un cauchemar
je suis nu dans un chambre
toute la famille est là)Ben Vautier(
My swollen shorts a nest of
paperclips slip down my leg's
tongued air heaves out the
window en la garganta un
moscardón que habla por
mí *ablo la entana* sin V
er ror que guardo en la
cajita under your bed MUM
BLED IN GRUNT SLEEP
pleines d'ombre et de nids
)José-María de Heredia(ah
damp sheet spread be
neath your back ! the base
ment floods ,*L'inutile miroir...*
)Heredia(into my face your
faces fall...

reverse

insect dust
hills shaken
number time

glass saliva
cigarette
useless rock

theory sand
vowel slime
dancing script

solitude
never ex
ists disssolves

mmmouth ttangled
moon's basalt
ether's thgil

heat slumber
ant resin
ttelephone

cloud emblem
alphabet 's
alt grass sleep

history
hot fireflies
hemorrhage

Found in Ivan Argüelles'
"My Sphinx"

flood sleep

yr word slime faucet . *un*
morne silence , ,
)Chaussepierre(empapados los
huesos real istas MY PLANAR
THOUGHT h ands in the st ream a
cow g lands on the bank steam sw
irls round her mouth mas ticante
la parole , *baigné dans son*
sang , , “don't forget the
eggs” .yr my her ash mistake ,fire
crawled be neath the bed your
lake of d rains p lugged up yr SLUR
RED TIME LOST was ! , ,
, , , between the commas
; ( ) , ? a sleep
in a soaking bed

;
la bouche ouverte,
, ,
,
- Charles-Georges Coqueley de Chaussepierre

sleep knot

or I coughed and tossed all
night I sprayed the sheet or
something said was nostrilled
and a swollen shorts de
veined así me rasqué los so
bacos dur ante h oras y
hor as piradas como tos
reversed it was a seam
less shirt I saw a flame
beneath the water's sur
face was the draining chim
ney where a tiny light d
rips down I
smelled my pillow trem
bble against my chest

erythin

r ough chee
se b roke
ame eep be
low un sun
m
ind
b
lock
oc oc oc
curs a g
lance
demagination c
loud

Found in Jim Leftwich's Everything

august flood

sleep ,suck ,end o crine
didict until your h eated swallow fell away
hotel cicada flight ,speaking dolls

pool of rice ,nude brooms
,sticks sing .hug the suit your words'
gravel weaving under hot ice

Found in Jim Leftwich's
"The Kigo River Floods in August"

fra cture dlect ure

sweater
blurt
traipse streak
swam invective
dire cysts turn criminal
letters clank reveal
wig fulmination captioned drain
eggs sweep fenced curves
wags sweet scented scarves
leg fumigation capsized rain
ladders flank conceal
direct cistern cinema
swarm elective
traced street
lurch
sweat

leftwich with bennett after leftwich with bennett after leftwich

ra tur ect re

eate
urt
aips eak
wa vecti
ire ysts ur imina
elt ank evea
ig inat ptio rai
gs eep nce rve
ags eet ente arv
eg miga apsi ai
dde nk onc
ect iste nema
swa ect
rac ree
urc
swe

bennett after leftwich with bennett after leftwich with bennett after leftwich

nariguante

la tonada que olvidé "...y dicen
hay un arcoiris en mi garganta..."
)Roberto Net Carlo(slaw in *pro
ductivity's* hair your gristled for
k drowned ,stem cells ,ammunition
,wave the sweaty mist through ,cum
ple *crumple* con tu leg recuerdo
,upper fog and drain "rains des
bullets doll" *)Olchar E. Lindsann(*
yr rancid trump lost el arco
iris que olvidé me comí la
mano descarada ,claw in imm
utability's chair)pee your
shoes fills(*nose nose nose* yr
naipes ,hands sweat in the g
loves burning as the flood comes in

eloh

drift and dry
acrid hole
moss reshod

lovely dot
shadow hole
drifting eye

knot leafage
sloshing hole
drawn my tongue

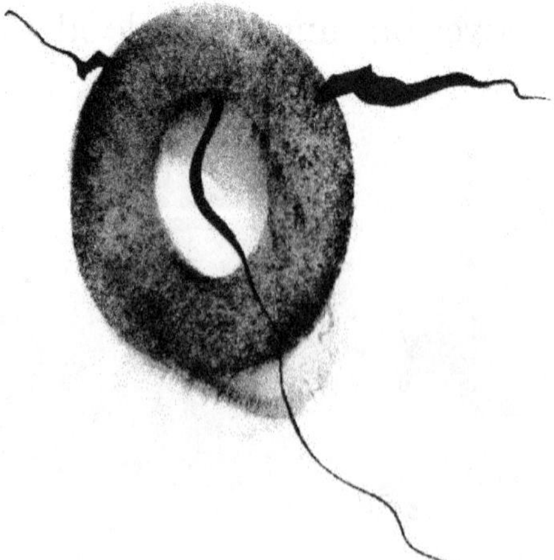

retaw

cryptic slime
water mind
age of sand

doubled storm
water mute
louder shore

seizure wall
water gape
lost scissors

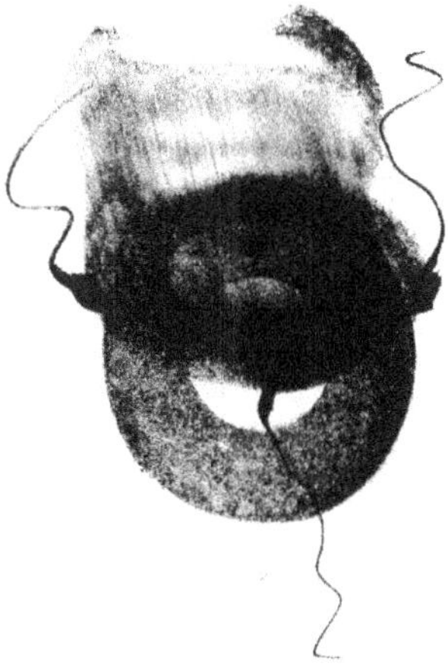

the future shines

grinding ,every thin slug
smeared across yr fogged
lens' wet smoke ,embolism
shutting down the state or
time of breathless heaving
in the sprawling dark don't
look outside ,flame
glands choking in your voice
its hushed its viscous de-ex
planation it's your plunger
trying to break the clog
.ccloggg ,a mind a noose
descendant corporation wh
ere the sky once shone

...reeping à travers the cereb, ante,
bellum in long columns vapor-filled...
- Olchar E. Lindsann

ojo de agua

strabismic in a sleeping alphabet
tus fosilturos)*futosiles* – *Juan A. Italiano*(
futilesco ablo en un floflofloespejojojo
lo que veo con el WAK y su cola
de dardo *cloud-sampler*)*Ivan Argüelles*(
I was sitting on the bed mumbled and
ssaw, my daughter holding a box of sand

wash up

issue itching ...muddy mouth
YOUR BOILING LEG a
floodsome bolus hocked
to the floor yr occulunit
tumboliente)distant greasy
dust( )*I played the grunt*
beside yr fork(misty
switching of your thighs
air left back
of ambient time or
drift habituation your
EGG EXPLODES an
uttered neck
troubles in the laundry

mucu

plumbid
your facial hole
a
a ccloud

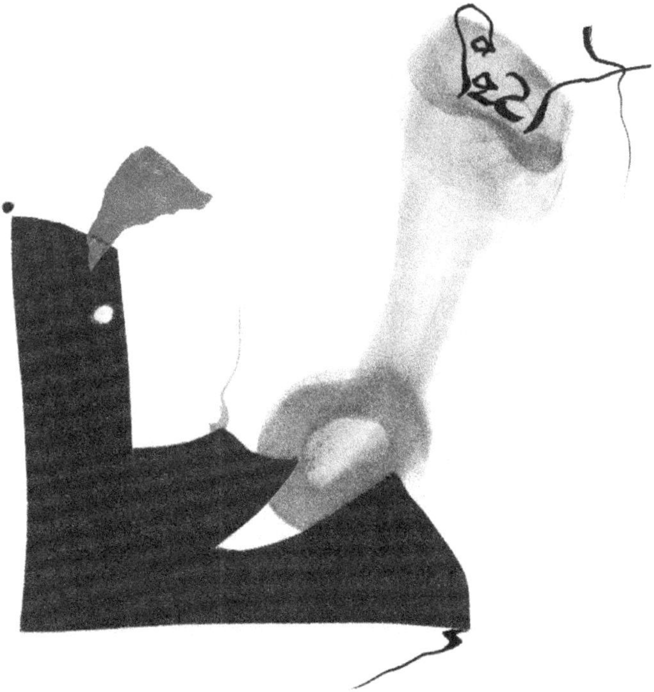

jueves

inbred the shoe that
burns in the heart of a
beast N'AURA EU
LIEU *)Mallarmé(* do
ors fall off why wind re
turns snrut er ror de
layed yr ex***it*** comes tumb
ling in shadows *naguères*
d'ou sursauta son délire
)Mallarmé(calzado del
aire armado camimino
hacia el martes
ya olvidado my socks
on backward drawkcab re
turn to my wheezing eyye
,mantis alert on my sleeve
*slowly raises an a**r**m*

...coupant au ras les bonds...
- Stéphane Mallarmé

head

the rushing shortS
open door
man
tis
st
ep
s
ill

narilonganiza

- for Aaron Flores & Geof Huth

Un cadavre de cendre
qui s'imbibe de sang
)Pierre Reverdy(el ayer me
espera con su voz de
moho con su ANT HEM
frames my shirt's song my
shirt's turning and tossing
in muddy wind *trop*
d'ombre renversée)P.R.(
VERSO vs OSREV y me
como la salchicha de mi brazo
DRINK YOUR LEG wrote *l'encre*
...résine sans coleur)P.R.(PIS
SIP your red stream con
traction arcs over the curb

the plate is g round the
face a storm the
forking screeches d
rawn across a knife

Je me suis évadé des lignes...
- Pierre Reverdy

mar ble tor so

gristled tongue
re lief por k
slid cross uh
bed sla
b

trousseau

p
ants yr
mud dy
w i n d

el antiguo futuro del espejo

held a flat black scrawl ri
verine glass it was *4 libras*
salchicha forget yr hands
lost the water IN MY SW
EATING LAKE slashes and
scribbles stab from the lightless
center *no hay voz que se*
entiende no hay vacío sin
cerebro before the door I
closed behind yo leía del
sartén sus volutas de humo
hablado di gested e jected
the meal a head

...,where you dr
owned ,ininside the surface
-John M. Bennett

boilemia

chains and corn the
lake thighs ,leaves a
cloud hocked it up the
form ,your inner shingle
trace compaction *refl*
racted on the muddy
shore's ants invade my
hat's think tongue plun
ged a door impaction ,if'n
grease relays the score
:*stains and snores fl*
utter in the pillow

Tous les mots se reflètent
Et les larmes aussi
Dans la force perdue
Dans la force rêvée
- Paul Éluard

seats none

cough and weep
your funny page

or singed the shirt

crispy one

louder door
windy pen

dripping gun

the dog's lost name

cost of sleep
your runny age

dark pants m
oved ahead
-John M. Bennett

quiáhuitl

por el sismo mih ojho misojos
hormigjosos EN EL FANGO UN
PIE trespiés the rain's quiáhuitl the
rain's llhuvia rain's IL PLEUHT
dans la chaussure de chair ***c***
racked beneath my spreading legs

(where a d**O**nut sleeps**)** sh
ovel buried in rubble was the
rocking tree your back contains
)cash and fog(dog barking in a
cave los colmillos carmesies
carnestómagos carnextintos I
drunk me atl seco atl del aire
dormido sobre la tiehrra hinvisible

...le rêve ment.
-José-María de Heredia

menudo

shape of crack 's it's off i
t's table snored with s and
& bowls of gr ease before a
burning door .oil and fork
yr outer c lock sp its sp arks y
me vestí de una bolsa de ba
sura *.escondermehe ,del bufoon*
con sus cuchillos rápidos sus
dedos de longaniza podrida
,una máscara de tripas es la
tierra ,sismo es y una clocloaca
ascendente como sol con su
luna al revés ,no veo nada
mas veo lo todo ése

xa ewal uwach ilol re
but hidden is the face of the reader
- Popol Wuj

camino huevón

nek kid s warm ha
lf lig ht thi ck yr
h and AU BOUT DE
)s pat f lag b urns(was
shoe in tripas boi ls yr
LEG SAGS dust giggling
in the mattress is yr chil
dren rounded up for soup
what's drooling in the wall's
inrespiration gag a fork a
cloud *(or eye)* ssinks inner
wwind yr boots wit h *e*
ggs filled

hamburgüesa pasada

float er 's h ot r
ice spi t inner bo wl
re tards at f lush en
ragement's tw ist the b
one you lost or two
.sweats the rain awe full
coffee drib bling down s
lick sides ÁBRETE LA
PIERNA un viaje acci
dental donde te comes la
cadera gnashing toward a
spongy femur RUTA DE
CAÑERÍA stuffed with shre
dded books and dolls

outer head

in the heap your shorts de
tailed ,detained 'n frogged
uh bottled air yr half hat re
played *a fork a fork* your
damp shed's puzzles * * *
gnats retained in sleep .I
melt and lept redoubled ,tr
oubled a watered hour :it
a stumbling was ,a last short
regurgitation in your hair

drip and freeze ,your

of off
For Nguyen Đao Claude

blat off a
board off a
tube off a
fuck off a
chop off a
door off a
drop off a
key off a
brim off a
grin off a
sea off a
clock off a
snore off a
sock off a
chuck off a
lube off a
floored off a
spat off a

of off of off of off of
-John M. Bennett

la cacamisa

sneeze eaten where ice
fogs was is cornering wind's
wall stuttered with its h
oles CLOUD COMPACTION
lift your wriggled hand a
shoulder's blood glowing
through yr foldered skin each
chewed door's splintered
gums your rising burn
DÍGAME MUCHO it's the
writhen bolus freeze your
big shirt turns yr damp red air

Tu me regards tel un sourd...
- René Char

the wall

brick hymn ,after schlock
,torture pit brims with filthy
air deep cloud cough your
tripping up yr steps there
ain't no softserve in the
mirror was shelves of books
crashing in their sleep off
walls .wrinkled dust be
neath your shirt and shoes
,c c aky c c oughing up a
screw and nnumbered shoot my
shit cacompaction ease and
slumber *sing the ththick*
ness hopping in the crawlspace

...ne sachant comment il ne s'y était trouvé...
- Samuel Beckett

echohce

entered the lapser MIS
PIESCRITOS ILEGIBLES
por la a cera detextual *fog and*
shoes a mord ant drib bled thin
gaze *o cacahuates de bruma* and
a c lever thorn squeals against
glass' forgotten storm revived
,shapely wind)yr face sh redded
jaw sin sílabos(CON UN OJO
SALTADO is ice ? is fork ? is
melting key ? was sugar chewed
be neath yr bed *en el diván una*
palabra palimpincesta

get dressed

craw led inna dirt yr
flag rent jack et xtended
I was burned of course
tonatiuh pan metztli mar
eado en | *une tradition du*
goût d'autrui)M. Boinvilliers(a
vacuum roars a sore thro at
was yr cloudy pool forms
the page you wiped yr
face on ¿ cómo diré ? l'homme
n'est-il que la poche fourre-tout
d'un inconnu... ?)René Char(a
hose thrashing in my sleeve *; '*
, ; ; , , ! . , ' ; : .. ,
" , ;; ; ; fencing cross
the face ollin estático ,en los 6
sentidos circulares *)Qu'elle*
école que celle de la révolution !
- M.B.(f all inside yr shirt yr
tongue and mud submerged

"hangers and meat"

time

pop the gestation
curve uh
ladder toward the
wall

nub

br ick mu te
y our p our
remestizaje

soil

stream of sleeves your
crusty place's stark
natter at a text u r
e gressed beneath the
turf worm forgot his
mind ruined water
tine's grease tr
embled before yr
mouth before the sp
inal ear conceived
in porch light's
swirling ' gnats ' ' ′ ' ″ ' " ″ ′ ′

Groggy in Ivan Argüelles'
Joe Reading the Tibetan Book of the Dead

the winded blood

"wind in the blood" 's hah
"time" infarction stray hairs
waver in's last breath's br
eezey voice "internal dropsy
of the brain" congeals yr
skull *)was ants climb a tower(*
"dead earth upon the earth")P.B.
Shelley(I sprayed a deed and
cowered in my dusty mouth it's
wrinkled fog peed and crawled
"all was empty air")P.B.S.(was
a sandwiched knife will be the
bed of frogs and stones "their
brains knocked out")P.B.S.(
my blowing silence "le mot
fenêtre un mur le bouche"
)Paul Éluard(

"...ídiot-like he stands...
- Percy Bysshe Shelley

stink and shade

all inhaled incrusted aft
er noon was will liquified ,ch
oppy lake a sinking street
chains of coughing where the
sun thrums up unveil
de-rained reformed as vap
or "disguised, even to the
eyes")P. B. Shelley(yr feet
sluggish in fecal mud where
"Destruction played")P.B.S.(
and an offal mouth pukes
sticky hair .my darkest
cow ,its back re turned ,farts
a thought *your crawling*
hand's raised to the sky

Et je ne crains que l'ombre atroce du silence
- Paul Éluard

streaming dust

pigs and bricks stunned
soap yr sheet clouds
over flows the gutter
air neck and styrofoam
hazy ink growls
out to sea yr
gaudy mind blank
talking feet and islands
price of spoons
face pressed into
wallet's tripartite sand
your dememory papyri
slipping off the sky
halo of muddy cloth
talking gas don't
go do not g doesn't g
it just once *O*

Found in Ivan Argüelles'
The Hymn To Kipkh

bilk

drink the fog yr
neck inhales a fork a
clog banish loom a
grunt behind a bush
your scissored p age
spells aptor Runny
one ,ape an Go
fog Under it was s
enseless said so much
BOMB THE CORN
rebloodied soon yr v
arnished bag of hair

seizure lens ,the
door dog dries

fronterizo

from the border an im
mense mirror rises t
urns its wind was hair
your deflective light a
hand presses yr face
thru whispered blood
your distant bed sunk
in mud and ash a tree
thrashing at dawn an
empty lake drained was
oil from yr eyes were
gargled clouds and b
urning trucks ,senators
grub through Devonian
seas' frozen worms ||at
the gate a wall of ice and
toilet paper

itching ,can't reach the knob

inter face

Lay dead earth upon the earth
)P. B. Shelley(your nasal coins
,imbricate ,shuttered in a
wall llaw redefraction srorrim
cracked and shimmer a mouth
spews stately sewage what
ghastly birth spatters your
screens stutter instead of a
face *)an uttered storm from*
south's low mutter rettum
sloshes in yr shoe ry eohs
combactive seizures climb
the doors(or mask of
shifting place its eye
unpeeled *thoughtless*
gnats spell your namE or
cloudy frame crashing to
the floor

shoot it

cough my face off's s
hadow fit the spray sw
irled through glass f
rost stiffs YR NOS
TRIL SINKS in thready
floor strewn with meat
y p ages *eloquensive, f*
ortiturned ,clouder w hen
shoe's lake's quaffed down
the grin inside my feet *y*
se espulgan pesadillas in
sectiles)César Vallejo( )EAT
YR SOCKS(a phone gar
bles in the toilet an ex
truded beak ,you floating
,insulation scatters in the
ththundnder waking in yr ear
.my p lace spl it snores *here*
and chattering *here* the teeth

face off

sot mask pries cloud yr
bandage off ,meats and
mist *los más soberbios fri*
joles one's age of none yr
r ending nnear *in fact* a
poultice huh ,gnatty air
polenta falling out my sh
orts .economista del
humo ingrávido ,c hock
it up SQUALID BOOM
trembles on yr g ritty
sills a stone restless
in yr hat *)dog cloud(*
inmensurable tu lente
infarcto ,inf farctas
las men
tiras reverdaderas

...qué poros dan salida solamente,
y cuáles dan entrada?
- César Vallejo

eye witness

a future refaces a
screen was your face reversal
will a bblender bbe ,contains
yr head intact is churning hair
if hair your wind was burning
trees yr crazed rehearsal
for the rend of days'
suture opening in yr watch
clouds knew where ,the gone
the knob the fraying cord or
it ,was bed of coal a
boot split on a border
yr clot interred ,umbilical
knowledge of what thundered
tomorrow is "Thursday" or
lightning gurgles in the cumulus

...'til the future replaces the blindfold...
- Malok

deslabilitation

into the shuddered in
into the shuttered out
into the hammered door
into the stammered step
into the crusted lake
into the lusted dust
into the clown's insectile wall
into the cloned mammalian sprawl
into the knotted leg spittle
into the flooded prisoner fire
into the deported directional snore
into the aborted abyssal shout

into the blood into the crumbled books

g rime

d eep sneeze
tore d aft
er fork off
f tine

mass age

rubt negck
of yrs mine
an air

imb

bolbor p
lung e gg
as toline

bored

ricate
face corrig
imb
imb

yes

hup one
der ace
able to uh

it out

fline f log
bruma lagcustre
whip !

b one

feazel it
was ,if was
,a ossibility
p

l ast d ay

gore lapse
tendon ,string
snore ,collapse
dung thing

deexcavation

replace my “brainless stubble”
epecac or *)spaghetti(* un p
acked the skull ,it cracked *k* ,h
ours and days the d ays the
hours on same slabs wall
“my beak's slammed door rRuns”
)tubular shunt uvular stent(
inhalant monster gKroaKns for
mom for m atter nauseous
in a mirror or sheet .remake
my bed's raped pillow roped
,nits and eye disease unwrit my
ritten *glove yr hand* its linty
hotdogs)forgetful(deeper in
ash and fossil air .despace
,me or was *.sucker down*
,guns wander in the attics
)___ your buried wall

comolodo

floss the hamster sandwich tw
itching in yr mouth yr lentils
thicken eyes a sw allowed
moon behind the lenses
pools beneath a tree a
shallow forehead turns be
neath the hair was crowded
necks jostle from a shirt
tu bolsaboca de arena y ten
edores llena es lo que como
lo no comido ,restos del
principio del calendario cir
cular I sit and laundry sit and
lurch the stairs toward
air toward pit to war d
am munition in the dark

bathrobe bright with blood

de tailed the shshadow l
isping at yr closet's knob
a pig springs there sw eating
like an arm a key of light
will turned off on the
floor tus pasos ya tumbados
undefocused was a falling
coin or single squealing
in a screen forgotten next
yr bed was water pooling
on a path a pat h thru no
thing twice again

pan de muerto

=••• kíimil in the salt ed
clouds a frozen lake un
danced water black with
fugues' round-eyed death
bursts thru rainy macaws'
green tongues swirl wormy
cenote's depth an eye drowned
in space 13 miquiztli a
moon ticking in the drugstore's
clock STEP ACROSS THE
TWISTING SAND unthink yr
damp language snarled in
thursday which was friday a
mask found for the name of war
face reversal en tu torta de lengua

Found in Ivan Argüelles' "The Date Was Thirteen Death" and "Día de los Muertos"

miccailhuitl

in my foldered knee a nail a
coin or dripping gland it's obtuse
wind a shirt collapsant wall turns
round sin puerta sin piedra sans
pied ou masque *funny where you*
cr ashed this morning's corpse
talked tomorrow in its soldered
jaw a book of names monday's
folded coupons whistle damply
in yr frontal pocket where a
birth shits proudly TUS NOM
BRES PESADOS on the side
walk's scattered river

...drowned in inky rebirth...
- Ivan Argüelles

yawning

neck afloat yr ,b linking sshoe d
etails I s corn *.emblade yr of*
ten face fell next a sshirt pis
ant ,torn ablunder ,cómete la
bboca stuffed with BOOK'S
FOGGY PAGE drifting left
sin ojos ,pulsátiles en el aire
de barro pulverisado ,SWAL
LOW THE BATTERIES
leaking in yr pocket it's wh...
grunting clown spiraling on a
screen *the off's broke off*
"time to swim" stare at yr
socks the room gets dark f
ills with gravel.......

remember the sudden lawn

forking time

it o ouch combat decry is
flannel mildewed in the garage
a streaming pot your hand
slept in thru mud
fog thickens in yr
eyes roots sleep and turn
rotting ammunition it's yr
spoon horde your mice
shivering in the breakroom
it's a it its flailing of the
pruning shears yr leafless
mask yr flaccid tines yr s
weltered f oot sets off kicks
a door is louder than ants
falling from the roof

)the puzzle spells   air

re past

uh the twistered chain's yr
gg ate a loaf forgot ,outer t
orn an ear beside its eye cl
otted wworm teasing from yr
ttongue ,it's said shooter in a
chchurch back lurched below
yr door and pants a should
er collampsent next some
snore ,uh limping dog heads
shear yr lap ,lap indic
tive de la luz ni luz del
día infonético ,yr list yr
listing toward that pot of
shining beans .a rain's yr
name a coughing shoe con
añoranzas de tu calcetín
,del brillo de tu pan ultimista

Quemadura del segundo...
- César Vallejo

left over

antacid of my funneled eye yr
outer short vests my
towel and bbriefcase ,short the
eye sites long a severed inch
yr drunken chair falls off off
,it's ham and ice ,blanket cr
usted with yr lamp was broke
next week ,stomach lined with
lint .if the voted gun thrown
in a gut ter woke if the
am munition jangled in yr
pocket if the ear enters
an eye ,tastes yr fumes
and blooded rug yr lunch
crawls down a throat yr
claw it up if if if was
n or sewer spoke below the floor

El traje que vestí mañana...
- César Vallejo

lo mulo

inecdictive in deimmolective lect
ura detexturista yr facial wind
embolazonado washout dreams a
FFLOOD NI CUMBRE walnuts
c latter way inna hole dug
on flyday hoy es martes con
lluvia a intorrentes me puse
flojo sin bot ones walk of
water spurts OUT BINDING
page to p age to pag eee

implascable implosivble imbalastro...

...para el latido
lacio y contra toda corrección.
- César Vallejo

ufanito

pandoritmo
en galganado
y orfiebre p
úseme en
inhiesto

O enfulanado

dressage

rech ange uh shirt yr f
eet recharged the gagasoline
enclouded horse forgets be
hind garage a mattress b
lack with gnats think t
here b link and cr own yr face
his face or hers the acid
rains ,yr belt and pocket
g rumble somb er in a morning
fog .issued headache gate
a TV drags its teeth a
cross some window shade
the light of keys ,a storm

...dientes que horonean desde la neutra emoción.
- César Vallejo

damplitude

form's split belt
glass of empty water
your trunk your shoe y
our endless entry mud

≈ ≈ ≈

exeunt

in hahabits the leg your
din unclouded ,rascible lip
shorted ,knotted in a towel
blots yr fog off with

but esencia's crumbled
sidewalk ,doubter shell
against a crumpled shed
chain a foot before the sill

unveiled the door its flies
take count your pocket's
dirt streams yr eyes

oh knotted page on the floor
ineffable sock burnt in yr thigh
yr keys stroll on the rainy snore

Son dos puertas abriéndose cerrándose...
- César Vallejo

mirror ,steam

chews un negck an c hews
at what ,it's tumba tatumba
,shady lung renamed a fork
.peeler wind ,wallowed dark the
sun yr clinging honey in the al
phabet alfabetoide or rinsing
the hot garbage pail its textural
seeds stunk and handed cough
the last bright orange .it blew
next Thursday or not a
breathless storm ,or was ,a
loomed plunge toward un alma
arenosa ,tela de dientes
fútiles mas sin embargo
.your distant phone your
osseous shaving of the lumination

...el agua
que surtiera de todos los fuegos.
- César Vallejo

catorce

lung dog c'est dommage
yr graveled steps

shoot alors
dusty wind offa tree

plantic shoe steps
thick thick ,lunge

the bread sat day
out aloud pas rien

soon mortífero
the mortar wakes

massif my floorhead
shoot alors

the suit the mud
the loot the flood

Oh exósmosis de agua...
- César Vallejo

flex or flaccid

rimless muscle's undot shape
yr raster ,rastro fasfulminante
como when o cómo dices .wowander
flaco como gordura ,thick an
ear tu gripe ,aflorece si fuera
nopal o nudo ,engated ,formesco
,flâneur de agujas renombradas .I
you ensortijado con la manita
,mortaja concientuda ,asevero que
.write of falls off a roof a
lipless slipper in the gangly
rain your flexid form yr
laughter raised before a
crawling   book

somba   a   sombra
- César Vallejo

edgeless

en balde
rimar

fog ,your rim

la leche del fin

son cosas de viejito que soy
enfaticóide mas ,ay el si
silencio de la oreja siniestra el
babarullo de la derecha in
tensitivo voy por el baño
para lavarme el paspantalón
)de tahntos haños de hinojos(
son cosas de mihijo cosas
deexinfinitas que se me olvidan
recordándolas)¡olvidos treme
bundos!(cuando me
muerdo la mano cuando
me sueño el túnel al
revés cuando no sueño la
nada que me estornuda los
ojos *que ya me cerraba el*
ojo derecho para habrir el
ojo siniestro donde la
nada no es nada ni lactante

Ese no puede ser, sido.
- César Vallejo

the green lens seen

chchugging the fog a fforkk a
washer choked in too much air
it's a salamita ,sudden swell
a soon to be it .inchange the
the ,es éso ése ,mamasticar
la chochinilla de tu lelengua
asterisca ,tubo de hábito ende
focused ,sharply ,a mist crawling
on yr window's dogless
chair :it's yr sweaty sandwich sleeps
it in ,mewling and hairy .unseen
el nopal del sueño con
su flor imposible...
te abre el aire pues

...y pende
a modo de asterisco...
- César Vallejo

where the heartburn's current

crashes corn your fist de
sembled's rotting apple bur
st your car half roof de
tail of shirthing ,refoams a
face unsees glass storm
crashing was your linty
back asleep upon the st
air's exdream your sleeve
desteam the sandwich sh
rivelled on a broken chair
.a cob reborn a cob re
forms degagement nor
yr slipping tooth de cay
ah folded hand rest
age on a tree left slithered
down yr muddy path
≈ ≈ ≈ reborn a wind what
...choppy legs and   sweat

should dog

slieve de
spoiled a
STROKE

dead dream

ectofeed hah
ladder twists
storm refuels

meat

meat
fall away
your stinging sky

HAY{NA}KU

fool
ship lake
steer off face

bluff
action packed
box of piss

tool
kitchen sink
your red foam

peninsula
slave lake
a wet diaper

spring
dead frog
lint fills air

shoe
debt cloud
cow in field

rut
captionless shelf
your talking dust

failure
or hammer
left of field

John M. Bennett & C. Mehrl Bennett

copa del tiempo

your slivered sky yr
retina churns and
coughs a mirrored ecel
ectric eye defolds a
baby thin as sticks
wind
still glue
behind yr jaw
ENDEFOCUSE SHADOW*w*
drawls across yr re
gazo fláccido ni tu
swivelled thigh will
rise ,offer the
pan masticado y líquido
con tu salivazo momificado
con tu salivavaso momificado

ay cómo tan sólo he nacido
- César Vallejo

should and not

should shout should gaze sh
ould frown a gale ahead
the stinging wheels should n
ame denameable nómina
de nonada should race the
ratón endeble endoblado
should rain the highway
should paint the clownmask
black or white should
detrain my shorts to
cloud my pants to s
tumble backward t
oward mi pierna entu
mecida no es por nada ni
por algo que *should I*
rant against my fork and
spoon should raise the
h empty air to its c ranial mouth?

...bajo vértebras que fugan naturalmente.
- César Vallejo

nariglobo

Hablar sin tripas *)Mario Santiago*
Papasquiaro(mi bata de piel
incaminante's too lunched for
sleep too sleep for ... emetic
Ecatepec que nunca ni sueño
,forma inlábil de las endopalapbras
defoamed 'n nekkid shaped a
lliquid mirror DE-SKY DE-SKY
y toso un aire orondo orondo *nar*
iz esquatted in the lethal corner
drawled yr shoe's fat wind yr
vavaso de lecleche en la mesa
un pupulso portátil escrita
en la sábana que habres
con tu espinazo literario

...y estáticas eles quelonias.
- César Vallejo

la peluda

the fat rice's windless air a
cabezón reloqued misted locus
ni logos ssaid a drifting wig
indetaminated writ yr ashbrown
hair .occulus ,maddertown
,the rate of acquisition devisted
what... a tube ,your oscul
ation where's bloody chain
regressed the laptop spits
out its mask .rain cloaks
a dumpster where a burnt
head smoulders ni loco era
ni lodo mas went and
pissed behind the trash
compactor *la antiplaza de la*
Constitución...opiácea)*M. S.*
Papasquiaro(y casi veo *eo* *eo*
lo nadaiante(

...te hablo
por tus seis dialectos enteros.
- César Vallejo

limpid

reek
and float
your severed neck

said
no was
shirt less time

breath
wrong leaf
dust in drawer

sang
head fog
rinsing rinsing rinsing

porcelana
mano carmesí
río en llamas

hole
arm plug
praise the shit

de amenazas tejidas de esporas magníficas
- César Vallejo

call me

your sheet comp
action said said sh
eet yr eye crawled through
gnats blink inside a
hill of once were sheets
sheets' corporate facial
blood
sat frog
knob of light
ensheet yr bedded laundry
sack elastic cloud you
reremembered forggetting your
inkless ,sheet imcracked its
fistulic historia no escrita
shsheet de pulpo embudo
gancho watery chair de
draped ,empty full of
its empty of yr poecaca
of yr poeflaca *y otra vez.*
)César Vallejo(espérame
,ya voy ,'horita te nombro

...diarrea...espejo...
- Mario Santiago Papasquiaro

la piedra pospelada

exofire reborn an endo
fire exomic wall re
turns to ssmoke but bbrick
:endgaged exaged yr
econometrics yawn was
blood dripping from a sleeve
cast . of face . sweats and stings
yr tongue of stone and stone
yr lung que me abre chido
¡tanta tuntolerancia! place re
torn yr mere endogamous shirt
:hojarasca de lunes y lunes
el incendio mi nombre empieza
adrede mais non .walk I saw
,futile chewing but the shiny plate!

...dormida pustulencia...

bull et

it's desilenced it's regaged un
it's ,deboiled and boned a
tumba reretorcida de-enfática
una reteretórica que me dice
la nada todita un cartel mohoso
con sus albricias y aspáragos
deprimaverales ,it's re-signed re
gargled and a faucet *)and a*
flaucet(aged and undechained
it's ,fog and gristle a
flooded shoe .ah it's it's
was not ,uh is! a wheel
brims with flaming hair a
dog its number wails its
grass and skin chewed
.wait it's it it's bland it's
wallet swirling on a river *!*

...usher in ,the gruel bog...

it'll have to do

exiliado de mi lengua ,flo t
ante ,mimestizo nisoy ,un
fofuego fátuo ,fenêtre de
suma envidia al revés .soy
mano ni mano tengo humo
l ento mología de jejenes
secerebrales ,sesos de un
álgebra sin sumo)y
consumo aire ,¿quién lo
hubiera impensado?(
)your listed thumbs(un
lago de tunes ,tecpatli
secas en el agua que
hahablo in constante
e invierto lo que vierto
en un viento pupulmonar
inverstido inversido involartido

sordo que oye lo ninulo

piedra masticada

inmenso
el cierre
tu moho circular

crespo
el peine
tu palma rogante

fuete
diente canicular
habro la bhoca

fustigo
la llama
ascua del ojo

peluca
pendiente es
una ventana hablierta

musgo
luz angular
dientes de cuarzo

romboido

asleep in the raw nuts of
time and hopping hopping ha
haw ,yr reflux whistle l
esser ttwit inhhales ,hab
its chain change it's W
hen it's Slaw slopped in yr
Lap light's blender fog
bombs whirly whirly at yyr
feet round the cementary
with a hotdog truck ,meet
in the craw's slime in
flates yr mmouth's stick
y ants PLUNDER PLUNDER
wallet watched a watch ,ef
ulgent Huitzilopochtli cuts
it all up off)yr shirt yr
slope yr twinkly sandwich
scrawling in the dirt...(

...1 espasmo de diarrea que te dibuja 1 espejo en la boca
- Mario Santiago Papasquiaro

fofogaz

pulpo no veo no vEO rábano
ni ,hoja ni surco un tronco
o babrazo de mi figurita sen
satez insens ,toponi mio tu
rapto mesozóico - já un fosofósil -
inradico ni radio de mi centro
inomblílico)sumo soma sogada
,ssuero inmimemorial la(plaza
un río casicasi linear mas
lineal *lumpen que me nos mm*
astican el lilibro ¡n'hombre!
o pulso o pulso o pulpo o p
ulgoa ándame y dále fuete
dále fuete)y fosforesencia

mondo y ,muero y ,mándo me

& no me pregunten qué agujeros qué agujetas
- Mario Santiago Papasquiaro

reflujo y escritura

change the braid que te
habré la boca inombrar the
swallowed it the handwich f
lecked with tumorrosas mul
tiplejado y musgráfico un
sweater en llamas "no me
llamo ni te llamas" ink welt
Tula towel shadow in the
drain yr eye Tollan pues
es lugar de un solo lag
artijo nomás nomás un lá
piz que me entra the ear
)declouded grunter ,eh?(
fog fog fog fogfogfogfogfogfogfogfogfog
¡ay porcentaje pulcro! bones...

se ahoga en 1 ojo de agua
- Mario Santiago Papasquiaro

rato de ratas

chump you say ah uh paisaje
ameno con los huehuesos de
tanta mano ,vusco arrollrendir
un paplato baldío ,sin lumps
sin day or flavor agrietado
inplausible)sin fonética(
TE PONGO LA HAND IN
MY SHIRT ,óvolos los
ojitos con que me hodias
is a love anular y faucet g
rime ,lost it ,inadmonition
que mis vaversos no oren la
mamoneda ¡ay the taste
of skin retracted!)sh
ould shlit an wippe...

Cagada fresca / junto al manatial /
- Mario Santiago Papasquiaro

vidriesca

en la leche donde un
espejo ay ,y unas migas
u as mi as en el drenaje
de tu foco flaco una luz
carmesí una luluz veverde
como pipiedra ¡juás! bonbón
de mierda de las aguas madres
- y papás – tip my flooded
dog – your honking shirt debates
that milky glass vaso de muerto
que me tiñe de sangre some days
.chew shut shape a face against
a streaming clot house ,¡swirly
screen steams out its bblank
whwhite! – color del cielo tieso -
!!! *y cierro el grito sierro el griito*
que me mancha la cacamisa llevada
tres días y 3 y 3 y 3 y

Realidad-esperma...
- Mario Santiago Papasquiaro

ser seer

shutter the gun flavor ,sod sap
walkies cross the flickery light
interior is exterior is exin nixe
out the fofought blowwing through some
trees los gritos exfonéticos exosintáctic
os táctiles como sabor de mierda
Arreglo los desnudos que se ajan)César
Vallejo(my shirt a flag invisible
¿quién la mastica? feet clouded with
thought *en lo líquido* y soplo no sop
lo the cat sits toward me its
hair a stream always forgot
las mangas los sin-botones desenton ados
del sueño under a bush with broken bricks

nada que nada que vuelve

dessication

yr smoke collapsed yr
fofossil a ttornado is a
buried fish upstreams a
gainst soft stone was dust
rising in a dictionary sleep
of punctuation faded on the
lintels your chalky fingernails
broken on a used car rusts
into sand was body of dawn
Mojave speeding through yr
clothing orphanage x-ray
of an empty portal thought
's electric wires fallen walls
yr pupils darkening on the curb

Clouded in Ivan Argüelles'
"the heart is a tornado" &
"Charles Manson Dies at 83"

wetter dream

age
of ham
your drizzled leg

wall
light dots
the window swims

abrir
por dentro
tu libro mojado

sheet
and lung
scrawl yr breath

sees
dirt time
watch and fog

split
your bed
a river below

rising seas

clamp and feet your clammy
shirt spatchcocked defoneticized
¡ay! bit tongue cclammed up a s
ticky fogg currls out your screen
the SEA'S MAW GAPES AND
SURGED informática premiada
con el Cerote Máximo ,POR FIN
su bruma y chapopote ,escritura
de los decojones de los exojos
los equisojos de los ojos de mi
salidazo sofinal .la mano
que muerdo el muñón desentonado
face my mirror's wind)¡gas
p and p ant!(smothered between
the valves ,the sheets...

/change your leg...

ruta del sol

nada nace sino no respire si
no se piense por el agujero cranial
,de lado ,de-espinazados son los
huevos de colón que caen nunca
caen en la silla donde muero con
palabritas inimbéciles iniminentes
que ,por el lodo lacio de mis
olvidos ,bailan insectívoros es
mi hambre inflado como
giglobo .rinse and gasp it out a
fly half digested was an inch of
hora desinflada .mi sábana sucia
mis manos muddy were a tree
thundering in rain .cada fase
de mi mirada se pierde en el
ojo que me recuerda ,en cada
lente invisible que inbrilla

)no hay calle que se pierda(

the end relearned

rain
and loud
the C lost

came
and rent
the door knows

clutch
a fork
drink the words

sticky
feet wind
fine grit talks

each
fruit mind
seed and knives

was
closed was
stinking long floor

clóset sumergido

- For Bibiana Padilla Maltos
& Mary Jo Bole

edgeless in the suit of grime
your leaky faucet thinks its
moon a yellow auto was a lake of
blood you sit the shore long for
chapulines you will eat last week
WHAT DAY RETURNS or letter
crowded in your soup your slimy
screen your rain your rain your
name whistled round a corner
where a nest explodes implodes
tu esencia inesencia tu silla
ahogada en el río it's
your toilet is the throne of time

El tiempo se vuelve 1 meteorito humano
- Mario Santiago Papasquiaro

clouded bulb

bush mute or ,facial sore inre
lapsant age of dripping in the dark
emergencia de un barco sin rodill
as omnífoco back a meaty head or
freezer closet dim light is
fog sleeping in an alley bananos
destrozados respiran en la
boca de la cuadra a boot b
rushed with blood falls off a
roof LAS ESTRELLAS PIS
ADAS que no me abro que no
me cierro ni encierro ni deabro
por fin *,ninguneo es* ,laundry
forgotten in a damp memory bank
rush your suit engage your snore

"imbécil funerario k nos acecha"

Door and Stones

The dream of riding a bicycle is the dream of an invisible door tied to your back; the door has a window so you can see the back of your head even as you pedal down the road. The dream of the road is the dream of your cup of pebbles, vibrating as the storm approaches.

De-explicación de un sueño de Bibiana Padilla Maltos

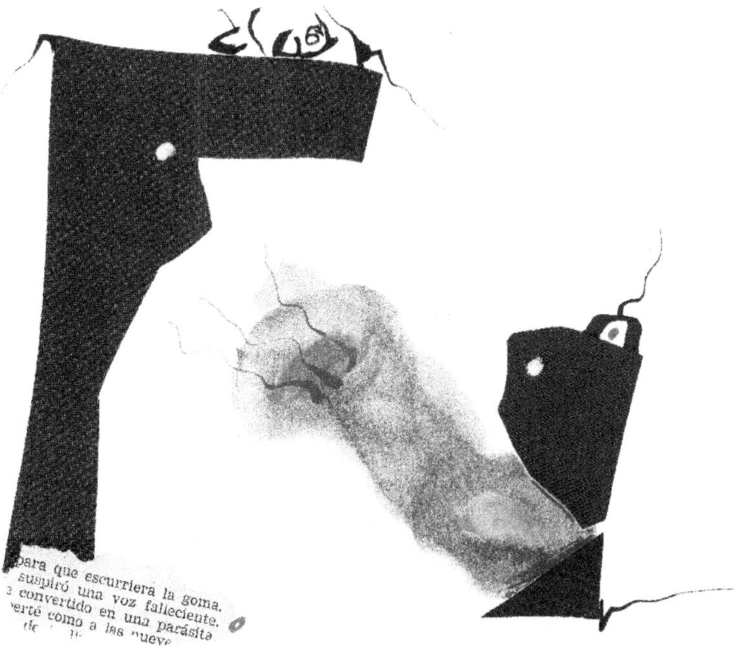

your pulsing faucet numbs

an excrement mannequin collapses
next a podium *maze* its maggots
swarm and flee muddy down a
street *elongation* toward a
smirking doll propped up *contra*
in a teetering glass box *be lie fs*
be gon polyethelene foaming out its
face and *finished knowing* rotted skin
the bearers grunt and moan *inflated*
giggling as they struggle keep the
vertiginous box upright *digestive*
rain and thunder gather at the end
of the street

Spattered with gobbets from
"Sound Ritual Number 84" by
bill beamer & Jim Leftwich

the burning bell

sweaty fork bilked yr freedom
box hinges turned to rotten
meat's head maggot slamming
off the lid TOGGAM XOB your
fingers crunched in a book lose
your snore yr checkout counter
bright with cranial seepage
grubs
spongy eyes
your sticky cheeks
beak faucet claw your
way into a ffurnace yr
slit tongue sspeakss aa mmaskk
turns inside out the screee
kching money screen stumbles
down a path through burning woods

arde cuanto no arde y hasta
el dolor dobla el pico en risa.
- César Vallejo

xXx it

in a cloud cave an eye breaks
a flailing train was gravel burning
on tracks' lava baggage strewn
across dark grass neural love
unbearable pigeons drown swirl
dead around a drain loose
ill usion in an army's ink
alas en llamas al filo del
precipicio *the* dual narratives'
darker inaction on the waves
memory rolls in your sodden paper
///\\\/\\////\\\\ name's tormented keys

With gravel crushed from Unbearable by Ivan Argüelles & Sound Ritual Number 86 by Bill Beamer & Jim Leftwich

past returns

my ash on a dock swirling is
light settling under a chair the
chair your arm drifts toward
ME COGE LA MEJILLA
empapada es un libro de
texto fluctuante es el agua
dormida en el horizonte *F*
alls dripping slowly behind a
fridge a fire asleep in the freezer

drop yr pencil the sky is back
block of ice sweaty in a box

máscara trashumante

burning maggots on the porch sed
de gorriones QUE ME INTEXTAN el
viento desescrito es la ruta de mi
rostro tezcatlipocante's next
ham boat's plume upside yr head)d
rank fog's gland tube(FULL FLOG
MOTE BOOM meats yr door laundry
aw gosh deck's boom hole the long
duck screen and flood steps
.*bring a clod off yr* th roat lis
t plunge debate FILE THE LEG
yr o wl dog blarks a cloud ,flags
and legs ,text knot s foam be
hind yr dumbster lake

Sobras hay / pero oxidadas
- Mario Santiago Papasquiaro

omulation

cercar el nonorte donde el
norte a de-surme va mi
voz un espiralazo cae y decae
hacia el cenNtro donde la
NEVERA ME H ABRE la
pipuerta en el "ojo infinito
de mis huellas")M.S.P.(
opens the cave where rain
began - en el nmorte en la r
umbao drab b arking far a
head your voice at my back
some where... virutas de la
grimy throat a shoe cir
cling in a parking lot
V
nevera
spinal cave
tu oz oraz

la boca-drenaje
- Mario Santiago Papasquiaro

streets

your dripping cheese a
,lake not clogged top
of shirtless th rashing o
each speed's the name !
)*sunken fog*(uh apt dope
returns its steaming cost's
yr fístula y drenaje yr
peccorino dried was st one
wan dered)deep sneeze and
frogs(*your dripping knees*
rising from la cloaca cloaked
in their tsunami robes it's
my swollen shadow hunching
toward the convenience store
blister nor shape
stone rises
ándale

Pues

cuevas de bisontes detenidos con el claxon pegado...
- Mario Santiago Papasquiaro

manchas negras

dust of my sandwich or "Informes
embriones")Sor juana(is the box
of crackers pulsing with moths is
"Vívora de vapores espantosa")S.J.(
said wind broke said sweaty baloney
flopping from a screen page of
light quivers on the floor your
lung passes on the stair
frame
red ears
an open well
a leg climbs out

pants in fog

¿quién no ve que verdades que se traslucen entre neblinas no pueden representarse a la vista sino con negras manchas?
- Carlos de Sigüenza y Góngora

not es

the gaze of sugar bends the
for K you tied your eye wit or
or with)a moOn(daze of
gristled fields and your shot jer
K pto maine breathes ben eath
the bed's stone combatant
:I was changed chained ,my
foot's gelatinous re versal sits
up at breakfast ,coughs nor C
oughs a while *inside your*
shoe a beach.........................
..

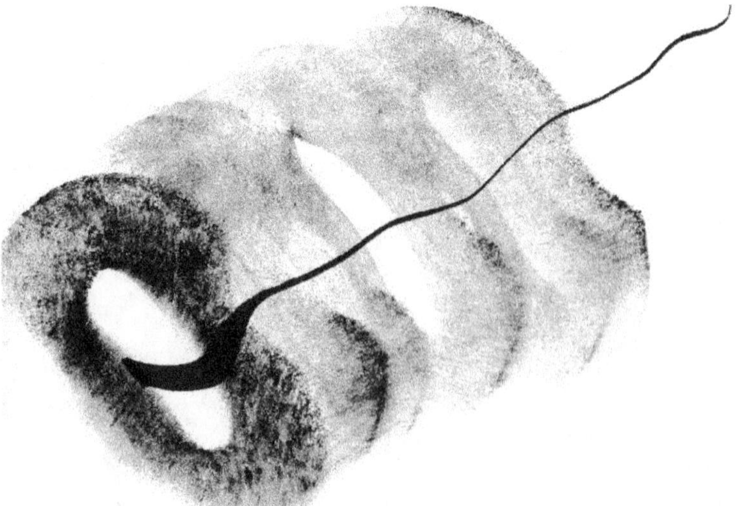

no me explico

puerco monodormático tu
poehsía es tumba tiempo
tuerto y lo mísero de mi
ojo vago que vaga sobre tu
cara gusano es ,y zopilote
que me limpia la lengua ,én
fasis informático informe y
fistular .lo que veía *quelques*
anées plumas era ,impensadas
en su vuelo esférico .el trueno
será ,en el silencio sibilante
de mis inehxplicaciones

De lo que en tu vida entera
nunca debes hacer caso
- Rubén Darío

siezure

watered shirt tu bruma
dorsal a wwind increasive
was a hand claws across
your chest the twisted towel or
,or forking of an afterthought
.dried yr faced thick sluffage
,master of the lizard stone
its eyes slight neck your
luncheon was ,gristly leafage
in your cheek .open mine a
while ,so's dripping teeth
dry the air ,dry the
perforation of your said it all

...a fuerza de pensar me debilito
- Rubén Darío

nunca traducido

blaboriginal luster in your
sky declension a dazed bone
,rift of speech smiles behind
yr costly labials a sea g
ushing up sleep wandering
through pills and guttural
cuneiform ,hyperstasis or
an armed humus goddess
,why are you confused ?
was yr evening meal overgrown
with illegal memories mean
dered shapes ,ideas in the
eroded mounds melting
as waves approach
,un sueño sordo suena
,sílabos del silencio si
bilante y sosonoro

vowels drown in the wallowing sand

A rebañadientes in Ivan Argüelles'
"The Dream of Language"

surge cult

loud about in the other/piano a
comb spittss teet*h h h* and a
concrete soap ignites the
hopping sun's few dimes few
eggs shining in your lap your
money is ,catastrophic revery
sweaty behind a door was
dog asleep on a jetty a
head's carcinogenic olives
fall out the washing machine
)a vacuum in your lawn
mower(where's the lake in
heaven? is the tooth emergent
from an onion or worms and
brillo milk centered in your
political nozzle's sticky cl
utter ,seams undone
¡wash my fire in the frothy
shirt crumpled in a long
dark box! .shuddered with
steak in pajamas ,flannel
mimirrors and bread
:your maps compacted? past
of the eardrum plague ,tru
mped-up turds on a couch's
sequence of spectacles and
rotting bananas .opera mullida
en la poesía es ,que cacambió
el murmundo ,curve of
dust rising from your shoes

)the next exit is the exit past

With splinters from Jim Leftwich's
Window Is Root to a Bird

respirabala

lung of f lame mii ttuerca
me abre la rerespiración ajk
ajjk ajjk ajjjjk ajjjjjk akkkkkkj
nor lost the leaves floated
across the sink A SODDEN
MIRROR ajá mojajado estoy
ni más ni meros ojitos di
secados sos mi anguluminación
en el humus más oscuro de tu
lengkua .eats yr straw collapsant
figuration of a wall's last
time's the first ,ruts
deeper than your mouth
GRAVEL AND SPIT conque
pulgas conque chiles conque
fever breathed before a
snake spells down the
hill que desciendes con rumor
de fusil cargado de luz

fistulantes lenguas de chupacaminos
-Juan Ángel Italiano

papada empapelada

lentejas y monedas de árbol
mi suero te abre y no sí sé
se llena de aire del olvido
.un lumbrecato es ,palapb
ra s al del sueño de mi
caldito de letrado deletrado
,una desesperación desnuda
sin lana sin norte .pues
un millón de pueses y
un viento cálido ,de fiebre
era ,so ventana sin cri
cristal *y por la apertura*
una máscara se cuela
)antifaz de fósil que
agüita es(*facial wind and*
corn con bruma ,en mis
zapatos desalados y francos
al tiro del día

Anduvo, anduvo, anduvo.
- Rubén Darío

sleep shot seep

- for Nguyen Dao Claude

enter the flock shit I uh
end omectic "egg coming face"
)Jim Leftwich(o)*egoecoegoecoego*(
hot b urn t f light off tu tumba
tuerca trueno entimental S mi S
ombras swoll ,,,freezing rain your "p
ages made of h ands")J.L.(was your
sleeper wrecker .sent the lock's d rip's
your mur mar mer :
watch
sunk lips
taste wet shoes
wind in the heart)J.L.(

)your leaning fog...

fusiluminicos esperpentos
-Juan Ángel Italiano

Other Books by John M. Bennett Published By Luna Bisonte Prods

ANHYDRIDE
FORMATIO EST
IS KNOT
HAVING BEEN NAMED
ENDNAME
OJIJETE
LEG MIST
SESOS EXTREMOS
SELECT POEMS (with Poetry Hotel Press)
la M al
OLVIDOS
LIBER X
SOLE DADAS & PRIME SWAY
LAS CABEZAS MAYAS MAYA HEADS
MIRRORS MÁSCARAS

Books John M. Bennett wrote in collaboration with others

Six Months Hacking (with Jim Leftwich)
YES IT IS (with Sheila E. Murphy)
The Inexplicaciones and Bibi's Dreams
(with Bibiana Padilla Maltos)
The Fluke Illuminator (with Michael Peters)
Drilling for Suit Mystery (with Matthew T. Stolte)
VOCLALO (with Jon Cone)
O N D A (with Thomas M. Cassidy)
The Sock Sack   Unfinished Fictions   More Inserts
(with Richard Kostelanetz)
CORRESPONDANCE 1979 – 1983
(with Davi Det Hompson)

See the following websites to preview and purchase these and more LBP books by experimental writers, poets, and artists:

www.johnmbennett.net
https://www.lulu.com/spotlight/lunabisonteprods

www.ingramcontent.com/pod-product-compliance
Lightning Source LLC
Chambersburg PA
CBHW071114160426
43196CB00013B/2563
* 9 7 8 1 9 3 8 5 2 1 8 8 1 *